T0276844

BROWN GIRLS DO BALLET

CELEBRATING DIVERSE GIRLS TAKING CENTER STAGE

TaKiyah Wallace-McMillian
Words by JaNay Brown-Wood

BLACK DOG
& LEVENTHAL
PUBLISHERS
NEW YORK

TO CHARLIE AND TRIPP, MY LIGHTNING AND THUNDER,
MAY THIS BOOK BE A TESTAMENT TO THE LIMITLESS BEAUTY
AND STRENGTH THAT RESIDES WITHIN YOU BOTH.

Black Dog & Leventhal Publishers
Hachette Book Group
1290 Avenue of the Americas, New York, NY 10104
www.blackdogandleventhal.com
BlackDogandLeventhal @BDLev

Distributed in the United Kingdom by Little, Brown Book Group UK, Carmelite House, 50 Victoria Embankment, London, EC4Y 0DZ

First Edition: August 2024

Published by Black Dog & Leventhal Publishers, an imprint of Hachette Book Group, Inc. The Black Dog & Leventhal Publishers name and logo are trademarks of Hachette Book Group, Inc.

Black Dog & Leventhal books may be purchased in bulk for business, educational, or promotional use. For more information, please contact your local bookseller or the Hachette Book Group Special Markets Department at Special.Markets@hbgusa.com.

Print book cover and interior design by Frances J. Soo Ping Chow.

Library of Congress Cataloging-in-Publication Data
Names: Wallace-McMillian, TaKiyah, author. | Brown-Wood, JaNay, author. Title: Brown girls do ballet / TaKiyah Wallace-McMillian with JaNay Brown-Wood.
Description: First edition. | New York, N.Y.: Black Dog & Leventhal, 2024. | Audience: Ages 4–8 | Summary: "From the photograph of the Instagram sensation Brown Girls Do Ballet and the author of The Color of Dance (BDL, Sept. 2023) comes this stunning nonfiction photographic book for kids ages 4–8 that empowers all children to express their true selves through movement and celebrate who they are while shining a light on dancers who have been underrepresented for too long"—Provided by publisher.
Identifiers: LCCN 2023042089 (print) | ISBN 9780762487592 (hardcover) |
Subjects: LCSH: Ballet—Juvenile literature. | African American ballerinas—Juvenile literature.
Classification: LCC GV1787.5 .W35 2024 (print) |
DDC 792.8—dc23/eng/20231018
LC record available at https://lccn.loc.gov/2023042089

ISBN: 978-0-7624-8759-2

Printed in China

1010

10 9 8 7 6 5 4 3 2 1

Brown Girl . . .

Yes, *you* there
with the thick curl in your hair
and the deep, dark hues of melanin
buried down within your skin. Brown Girl,
you were born to take that stage.

Brown Girl, b e n d—
your knees, elbows, neck—and send
awe through each of them so blessed
to witness you in motion,

the vibrance of your beauty
as it glows and grows and flows

from the top of your poised crown to
the tip of pointed toe.

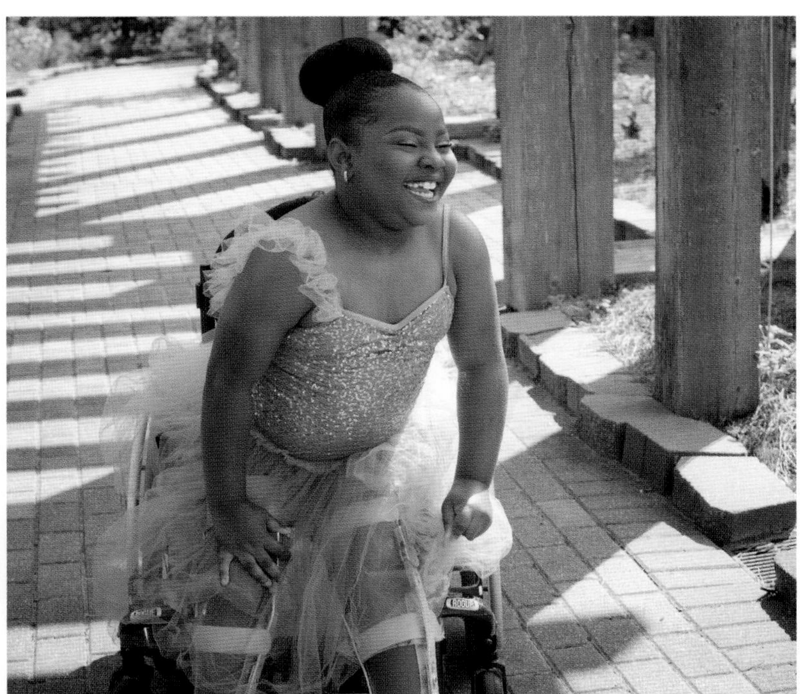

Do you even *know* the power that you hold?

Set the stage aflame while you plié!
Then elevé!
Go on, Girl, sauté! Sway!
SLAY!

Now stretch and twist and
leap and keep
that magic burning brightly

as you lift, you reach,
you shine like light—see—
from the most luminous of stars.

You are fire—
a vivid bird taking flight.
Dance, Girl!
Show the world your Brown Girl glow.

Let them know
that you belong at center stage.

Pirouette, glissade, passé—
keep the crowd with bated breath,
bloom and rise, split through the air
and take them to your gran jeté.

Let them gasp,
wowed by all your
magic.

Golden glitter glimmers on your
glistening skin,
reflecting spotlight.
Brown Girl, you were made
for front
and center.

Paint a picture with your
pointed toe.
Tell your story with your
motion—
wave of sinew, swell of muscle,
poem of body mixed with music.

Let your poised and
postured movement,
leave no doubt.
Do not doubt.
Ballet was made for you.
And you were made to dance.

So,
tie your ballet shoes up tightly.
Slide into your leotard.
Pull your tights taut.

Coif your hair high.
Practice till you and your moves are one.

Then turn on that Brown Girl flair.
Let it drown out any skeptic, Girl,
your magic is electric,
take your place there on that stage

and Brown Girl,
DO BALLET!